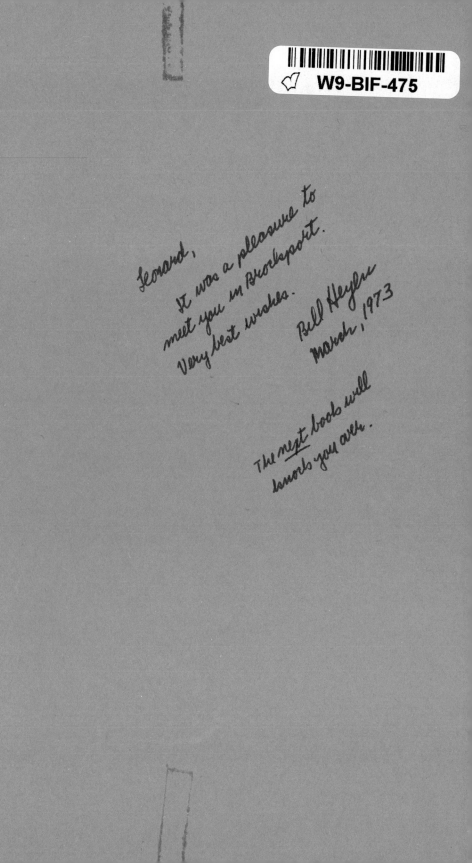

Leonard,

It was a pleasure to
meet you in Brockport.
Very best wishes.

Bill Heyen
March, 1973

The next book will
knock you over.

DEPTH OF FIELD

DEPTH OF FIELD

Poems by William Heyen

LOUISIANA STATE UNIVERSITY PRESS
BATON ROUGE
1970

Many of the poems collected here first appeared in the following publications, to whose editors grateful acknowledgment is made for permission to reprint: *American Scholar* ("The Bear"), *English Record* ("Indian Summer"), *Four Quarters* ("Somewhere, Another Continent"), *Minnesota Review* ("Loch Ness," "Prose Poem"), *Modern Poetry Studies* ("In the Asylum," "The Dead," "For Hermann Heyen," "The Stadium"), *New Orleans Review* ("Windfall"), *New York Times* ("Birds and Roses Are Birds and Roses," "A Man Is a Forked Animal"), *Ohio University Review* ("The Exhumation"), *Poetry* ("Kamikaze," "Depth of Field," "The King's Men"), *Poetry Northwest* ("Existential," "The Deer," "The Dark," "The Doors," "The Mist"), *Prairie Schooner* ("Boy of Gull, Boy of Brine," "To Live in the World"), *Quarterly Review of Literature* ("For Wilhelm Heyen"), *Shenandoah* ("I Move to Random Consolations"), *Southern Humanities Review* ("The Mind as Green Thumb"), *Southern Review* ("The China Bull," "In Memoriam: Theodore Roethke"), *University of Windsor Review* ("Contingency," "Gravity," "Winter Solstice"), *Western Humanities Review* ("Postcard," "Prelude to an Epitaph"), *Wormwood Review* ("The Sacrament").

The author wishes to thank the Borestone Mountain Awards Committee of 1966 for the prize given to "Boy of Gull, Boy of Brine," which originally appeared in *Prairie Schooner* and subsequently in *Best Poems of 1965* (Palo Alto, 1966); also, the State University of New York Research Foundation for two fellowships which led to the completion of this volume. And thanks to Belva Browne for all of her typing.

Library of Congress Catalog Card Number: 77–108200
SBN: 8071–0932–0
Manufactured in the United States of America by
Kingsport Press, Inc., Kingsport, Tennessee
Designed by Jules B. McKee

For Han, my wife

If I ever see more clearly at one time than at another, the medium through which I see is clearer.

—THOREAU

As a blind man, lifting a curtain, knows it is morning,
I know this change:
On one side of silence there is no smile;
But when I breathe with the birds,
The spirit of wrath becomes the spirit of blessing,
And the dead begin from their dark to sing in my sleep.

—THEODORE ROETHKE

Contents

DEPTH OF FIELD

I

THE SPIRIT OF WRATH

These
moments,
half-
awake

and half-
asleep,
half the light
of a dream's

windows
trailing
off,
and half

the light
of the moon,
or sun,
silhouetting

the shades,
or the lids
of your half-
closed

and half-
opened
eyes;

neither in
nor out
of any life;
your pulse

the slow
beat
of a frog's
under

the mud,
under
a roof of water,
sky

of thickening
ice;
you move,
or dream

you move
to a window
to lift
a shade

to watch
the breaking
dark.

FOR WILHELM HEYEN
(*d. 1940, buried in Holland*)

I

The shaft of the film curls with smoke.
Within the camera's depth of field:

battalions of bone-white crosses
(the lines of a chaplain's gestures

in a pre-battle benediction)
and a still-living soldier

fronting them, and staring
into my eyes, into the dark. He waves.

The soldier moves his right arm.
This is, and was, certain in time.

II

The film shakes, and holds.
He chars at the edges, and burns,

but the film moves. Holland
is snowing. Trucks

lumber like polar bears.
Soldiers are digging trenches,

stacking shells, stringing
barbed wire with cans, planting

mines. Night falls. The wire
rattles. The mines flower.

III

Because the cause is never just,
rest, my Nazi uncle, rest.

All the oppressors are oppressed.
The dog's heart is his only beast.

I say you walked with soldiers,
killed, were killed. The Dutch

tore the medals from your chest.
The book of lovers' poems

my father said you pressed
out of your heart is also dust.

IV

Wilhelm, your face is a shadow
under your helmet,

fades from the granular air
of newsreels. You cannot hear

your nephew try to celebrate your name.
I've seen you move your arm

like a scythe, a pendulum,
seen your hands cupped full with blood.

These are all your wars.
Asia trembles. You are never dead.

KAMIKAZE

Their scarves moving
in a gray, pacific wind,
in the dim, shadowy motions
of celluloid, in my dreams
of Asian gestures spinned
on the vague, unsequenced reel
of my heart (destroying
shapes in the dark water,
or destroyed, flaming
meteoric through the dark air).

Sweeping the divine wind
into their full lungs,
breathing the ocean's air.

Being every war's
valorous dead, draining
their sweet destiny
with a last cup of saki
and a kiss, meeting
the all, inevitable sea
and the incessant film
of my dreams with eyes
already beyond death,
chests brass as the rising sun.

Seeing this, knowing
I will never fully escape
from such pilots.

FOR HERMANN HEYEN
(*d. 1941 over Russia*)

Hermann, the Channel was blue-green
when you banked your plane and headed
back. But the Stuka's wing,
down which you sighted the countries you hated,
shone brilliant as medals,
didn't it? Your plane seemed
almost to be on fire, didn't it?

Hermann, you received the letters
my father still talks and wonders about—
the ones in which he told you to bail out
over England and plead insanity.
You got the letters, didn't you?
You kept saying you'd land in London
with the rest of your squadron,

in a few months, when the war was over,
of course. Of course. But they needed you
in Russia, didn't they? And the few
who bailed out there were met by peasants
with pitchforks and scythes, weren't they?
Anyway, your plane blew up like, for a moment,
a sun; your dust bailed out all over.

Hermann, I don't mean to make fun.
But this is only a wargame I'm playing,
anyway, isn't it?—pretending you can listen,
or that you matter any more.
In any case, this is what happened
past the days your ashes sifted
down through the gray Asian air:

9

the Allies leveled even Berchtesgaden,
where, released, your warlord's charred bones
sang hosannas in their sleep.
Hiroshima, and then Nagasaki collided
with two suns, and this probably ended it.
(Men were blown dead as the shadows of clouds.
That war passed on with the wind.)

Hermann, what would you say now
if you could talk? How would you deny
my father's letters? I keep
questioning him. He says: *Ich habe ihm oft
geschrieben, aber* . . . . He is almost sixty
now, and begins to miss both you
and Wilhelm—who is buried in Holland, by the way—

more than ever. Your living brother's heart,
so to speak, has empty corridors.
He sleeps back to the day Wilhelm
was killed, and the day you burned,
for a moment, like a sun. He stares
for hours at old photographs
of the two of you in uniform.

Hermann, my three brothers and I
are the most dispassionate of all Heyens ever.
Though named for Wilhelm, your poet-brother,
I often curse the two of you and spend my hours
writing verses that wonder how your fiery,
German romanticism started,
and where, at last, it died.

BIRDS AND ROSES
ARE BIRDS AND ROSES

I have come to rely
on the timeless in the temporal,
on the always faithful inner-eye,
on detail that deepens to fond symbol.

But all morning the sun found
feathers scattered under a bush
where roses had fallen to the ground.
The remains of a thrush.

I would flesh this one bird's feathers,
resume its quick eye and lilting trill.
But these were not the mystics' flowers:
their bush cast a shadow like a bell.

I

Off Crane's Neck the sun
reaches a few feet down
into the dark water,
but what it is you're after

feeds at the bottom
below the reach of your anchor.
Your heavy-test line
plummets with its lead sinkers

down deeper than Twain ever
marked the depth of his river,
and strikes sand
with a slight thud and shudder

you feel in your fingers.
The line bows out. The sinkers must
touch, lift, and touch again,
raising swirls of sand,

trailing smells of the squid
hooked higher on the line. You drift
in swells, as though the Sound
drew breath beneath you.

II

As you wait for shark, remember:
from here, crossing to Connecticut,
Walt Whitman saw poems,
watched the small boats troll

for striped bass, for blues
that bent rods double,
for porgies that shimmered
in the sun like coral.

But you've reached deeper,
down to where the sandshark cruises,
glides among the dunes like a shadow,
slashes anything that moves.

Its flesh, cut in strips,
will quiver, like a turtle's, or snake's.
Its eyes will stare through you, focus
beyond you. Its teeth

can snap off the neck of a bottle.
You'll feel it strike,
hook itself, sweep your line
back and forth under the boat.

III

Hold the line taut.
Reel the shark to surface.
Gaff its white abdomen.
Raise it to an oarlock.

Batter its head with a hammer.
Taste the blood that runs
from its gills, hack off its tail.
Draw your knife across its eyes.

You've done what can be done
to the snarling shark that still
moves like a dead snake until
the sun dies beyond the horizon.

Rip your hook from its gullet.
With both hands, hold the shark
above your head. Pray:
never again to fear the dark

sea's depths. Pray: *never to fear
yourself.* Pray: *never to fear love.*
When you lift it back to water
the shark will swim away.

A MAN IS A FORKED ANIMAL

A horse does not think well enough to know
his waking from his standing sleep,
his fields moving their grasses in the sun
from his dreams of fields,
stars from the points of fireflies
under his staring eyes. He walks
from one sleep to another, never alive
within the tension of his weight.

The door of the stable closes, or opens;
the great roof falls into darkness,
or bursts with fire. It is all one.
Windfalls shine as he nods in his stall.

THE BEAR

I

I was the first of us, leaving a downtown bar
one spring dusk, to see the bear.
I blamed it on beer.

It crossed the street to my side, deeper black
than the shut shops or near dark.
I tried to blink it back.

It passed an arm's length away. I stood straight
as a parking meter, and could scent
its long-slept lust.

I was the first of us to see the bear, the first to follow
its musky, rutting smell like a shadow
to its spring lair.

II

The beast's eyes glowed yellow on the stairs.
It rose to two legs and ripped its claws
across her shut door.

She led me quickly across her room, and bade
the enraged bear stand guard
beside her bed.

She pulled me down, and all the while
I felt its hot, fragrant muzzle,
until I heard her call

another to step inside the cage, the first to follow.
Later, the magic bear slept. As though
it could ever sleep another winter.

Walking the small oval of Gibbs Pond,
scaring the leopard frogs to jump
and the snappers to swim out to darkness,
watching the emerald and ruby needles trail
their frail legs and copulate hovering in air,

noticing the black spiders stride their shadows,
I came across within some razor weeds
some sort of crane that came to die.
And I, kneeling beside its quick rising
and falling body, seeing the ants
had begun crawling its stilt legs
to its moulted sternum and sad, lidded eyes,
took up a death-watch with the rising gnats.

I was at first no mourner, but a scientist:
soon the bird folded its right leg to body;
in one hour it lay down, in two, closed its eyes.

By last light the frogs had again begun
and a snake had wriggled to the shore
and flicked something to its pink tongue.
A turtle gnawed the belly of a fish.
But, being less objective than I'd wish,

I rose to rock the crane's death; and, needing something
to affirm, held to the knowledge that a bird's beak,
born of cells of bone, discourages the worm.

THE MOWER

No more stars are slashed from the hive
of heaven. The evening settles to stillness.
Today the wind's edges swept
the orchard like scythes. Now she rests.

Now the power mower,
drowsing in fumes of gasoline,
though all day her blades whirled
through windfalls under the apple trees;

though she was the great queen to bees
that rose from burrows in the fruit's flesh
to preen for her, to hear
her droning epithalamion;

neither dreams in her dark shed
nor sings mass for the dead, whose wings
are a scatter of stars on the cut grass.
She mows and rests in mindless monotone.

WINDFALL

Because it was there, tasting the wet morning,
hearing the air with its tongue; because it coiled
to a half-cone of rope, and tasted, and listened;
because it was there, and I was harvesting:
I hoed off its head at break of morning,
draped its body over a branch of flowering dogwood,
but the whip still moved, jerked and swayed
like a vine in the scented breezes of evening.

Another pink, dim blossom, but long-lived,
the flesh stump of its curved neck swung
(as though its eyes still held it on a string)
and wouldn't stop. It wouldn't stop. *It would:*
I found its staring head, and stamped, and heeled.
I didn't know why I did it, but I did.
Then the wind died, fell from the tree, but laden
with none of the promised, eventual fruit of Eden.

ON THE THAMES

Ice is already gathering under
the robin's orange tongue, and we,
watching the leaves fall like old men's hands, wonder
what we'll do and where we'll be

when summer comes around again.
We can't put our fingers on it.
Nothing we can mention.
Nothing I can arrange in a sonnet.

We shut the stove down.
The pilot light extinguishes
its thin, blue flame. I watch the sun
fall while you pack dishes.

Between our property
and the creek we named the Thames,
a single tiger lily
insists its orange flames

above the weeds. O what they'd
have done with this freak flower
blooming in the shade,
the old masters!—wrung out the last sweet spark of splendor

and glory!—But our generation can't do it,
can't sing the mystic flames. The sun races a colder
sky and can't burn through it.
We and our world have gotten older.

EXISTENTIAL

Half seeing and half smelling a scrap
of bacon, an eel blunts its nose on wire,
but finally steers into the cone of water
given shape by the trap.

Eats, and begins to define the rigid walls
of its cell. Burrows its mud floor, but bares
the same wire. The eel hovers, stares,
circles and settles.

It hears its gills feel the waters flow.
Waits in its cage. It can't or won't remember
the small way out it entered, or does know
and doesn't care, or neither.

CONTINGENCY

*A cosmic ultimate, . . . the
causal intersection of two or more
mutually independent and pre-
viously unrelated causal series.*
                    —CORLISS LAMONT

Over the city
a gull's heart stops
in mid-air.
The bird plummets
in gusts of wind,
its light bones,
the lift of its limp wings
now canceled and now not
by rushing air
and gravity.

Hubcaps scrape
and settle.
Later, a witness finds its feathers,
bits of gut on the glass.
As though
there were a common law
that drew the car and gull
together there, he tries
to understand, stands
gazing at the skies.

I

Its gaudy colors out of place
in the dull sand, a child's pail
points like an eye to the race
of cold wave to cold shore

and a single dirty gull
ruffles its feathers tight
against the wind and keeps in sight
a lost season, and a ghost.

There are other images
of a nether, warmer, slower time
of year, vestiges
of summer, echoes of a small boy

with a shovel and a bright pail:
a weed floating like a scab;
the empty shell of a spider crab
that made him run and laugh

at claws, or at any kind of web;
the torn wreckage of a paper bag
caught in a sure ebb
of tide; the shuttered pavilion

that felt his feet, and more:
the winds and cloud spurs;
the driftwood he piled, like antlers
from long-dead stags.

If water love the very young,
let it take one horn to him, and this pail
of color. Let the ocean's tongue
be warm and the fish kind to his wail

for this is holy ground
and water for gold urns.
For this is where the sea turns
his body where he lately drowned

in the dazzle of white waves; here rain
and snow will plant his early grave
for a thousand years. Save
this song, you gods, and save my pain

as testament of love
for a lost son who suffered
under the sky, was sepulchered
by sea, and rests. Above

the crucifix of years this hymn
be sung in sorrow, these words nailed
to ages, though a father failed,
through tightened throat, to honor him:

Boy of gull, of brine,
of crab and gray wave,
of love, of waterdeath, of mine—
be hallowed in your grave.

Madmen stuff their ears
with cherry pits. These root,
leaf, and bloom.

Blood beats like sap
until the trees stand, complete,
inviolate, and lovely. In this country
nothing, no one

is undone by beauty.
The trees never lose their fruit
to shrill starlings, or rot, or insects
crawling from tents

of web. Remind them
of Genesis, the verses that tell
of the protean snake that spoiled Eden.
the inmates will smile:

their trees shimmer
in light rain. The lost world
is theirs again.

PROSE POEM

Just once, allow me to tell you,
without illustrations, figures, pictures,
what your life is.

First, you are the only one alive.
This is what you feel,
not what you think.

Second, you do not feel
there was ever a time
you were not alive. History

is bunk. Plato never lived,
or Christ, or Thoreau. They struggled
into your dreams, extensions,

your own imaginings,
inventions. Third, you will never
die. There will never come a time

you are not alive.
This is not what you think,
not what your mind, which seldom

knocks against this knotty wood, thinks,
but what you feel. I mean,
your heart is here to hold sway,

defend you from the Lord of Zero.
Fourth, and finally, you've read these lines
thinking: this was written by a madman.

THE INSECT

It never touches earth
though some say its legs
reach down just to the treetops
like rays of the sun.

It is transparent and takes on
the colors of the sky.
At night it is black. Stars
shine through it, the moon

draws it back and forth
like the tide. You have heard
the song of the wind
passing through its wings,

but cannot see it
as it floats above you
gliding on airstreams forever.
And it is huge. A plane

can pass between two cells
in its eye, a bird can fly
under it from morning to noon
and not pass it by.

It feeds on dust, woodsmoke,
blue clouds of vapor that rise
from the forests, everything the wind
carries. It never sleeps,

never tires, never dies.
You have thought its white shadow
moving across the ground
was the shadow of a cloud.

You have always known this.
You have always known the insect
is there. You are always
about to say its name.

THE SPIDER

The spider hovers always
just above the land
and when it walks
your pulse quickens

and where it walks the world
grows silent, birds
abandon their nests, deer
rush headlong across the roads, mice

burrow deeper, even the wind
seems to die.
The spider is white, its legs
like rain lit in shafts

of sunlight. The spider spins webs
like the sun spins them
under the water. You have seen
its nets and vines of silk

swaying between clouds,
almost invisible, almost unreal.
You have mistaken its breath
for woodsmoke, its body

for a snowstorm on the horizon.
For once, enter the eye of the spider,
see what it sees, wait for
insects bigger than islands

to strum its web. Fear
what it fears. It is summer.
You are the hunted and the hunter.
But you are not alone.

Many have seen the white fur
in the joints of its legs.
Listen. The spider is poised
in the air above you.

Caves in the mountains of snow
where men disappear,
in the hooded Himalayas,
and caves in the mind

where he lumbers,
the Yeti, snowman, like a tree
shagged with crusts of ice,
his fur matted, his eyes

far back in his head.
Some have seen the foul,
brown huffs of his breath
in the mountain air. He turns

away, his shape like the blue shadow
of dusk, his tracks filling
with snow. Some say
he is a bear, but no white bear

lives here and rears up
on two feet and roars higher
than the pitch of the wind.
But some (listen to them)

will tell you where to find
an old man who squats
in a trance and stares at the grail
of the Yeti's skull.

Find him. Sit down beside him.
He will light a candle
where the dim brain burned.
The Yeti's eyes will dance on the wall.

I

They know, the neighbors of Loch Ness,
what rises, treads water in the dark,
bellows, bellows. Its neck curves,
a cobra's, scaled; its eyes burn with,
its jaws snap at the blinding moon.
This is the creature they turn with
from sleep, hearing it break surface
now. This is the moment. Now.

II

There is a card, its background black,
in the Tarot deck. The nine of swords:
a sleeper has just now wrenched up,
bends double in bed, has hidden his face
in his hands. . . . Oh, yes, we all
hide wolves in the caves of our hearts
that bristle when the moon burns, pad
to the crags of our bones, slaver and howl.

III

But ask the neighbors of Loch Ness,
who have had nightmares, awakened
to wolves. They will tell you this:
wolves are one fear, the lesser.
In the beginning, waiting, there was out there
in the dark water something outside ourselves
Noah never—it swam beneath—harbored
in the hold of his ark. It does not die with us.

II

THE DEAD FROM THEIR DARK

This evening's damp air
mutes even the crickets
used to scraping such shrill music.
The grass has fallen
almost to full dark.

I walk through flowerbeds,
inhaling the mixed perfumes
of black loam and moth-white mums,
through hedges to the row of dogwoods
blooming above the lawn:

their wash of pink blossoms seems
to float them in fathomless water,
like Monet's last lilies,
or Melville's rootless meadow,
through which whales swim like scythes.

If this were the way the dead lost ground,
if the dead were drowned
if an evening's hushed, heavy air,
if the eyes of the dead branched
with an orchard of pink coral . . .

If this were death's kingdom,
if the eyes of the dead were not
a colorless blur,
if their blue bones
hummed beneath their stones . . .

Somewhere the May skies
rumble with thunder, flash
with edges of yellow lightning.
Something is about to happen,
as in the best paintings.

From the pond a field away,
bullfrogs croak to their log king.
What was it I
was thinking of saying?
I can't remember.

IN MEMORIAM: THEODORE ROETHKE

I

A gourd like Jonah's, brimming with dark, still water,
hangs from a rafter. No wind quickening
to sway it loose from its shade.
Becoming, it is breathing
only mosquitoes rising
from small fish.

Nothing has moved for so long,
his flowers are drowsing in my house of bones.
I need his river's undersong.

The wind is trapped in the mouths of flowers.
The morning glory folds its victrola shape.
The dog sniffing the vines dies among the briars.

O Lord, send
your worm,
a storm.

II

If the stations are dark,
the porters gone,
the platforms deserted in the dead of morning,
the rails flowering with rust,
the trains gathering cobwebs in their sheds;

If the busses are lost in the woods,
the roads pitted and crossed with fallen poles;

If poisonous fogs settle in empty hangars,
the planes all abandoned in far fields;

Whatever cripple seeks a Lord,
however slowly,
a Lord finds.

III

Theodore Roethke, once locked
in a glass house, is dead.
He heard a low sobbing in the veins
of small things, a sucking to live.
A trapped lark cried love, love,
from a dripping pipe.

Overhead, over the flats of roses
(his blood warming with the breathing dirt),
over the slanted panes (the first eyes
of a child's adoration), the great bear
of heaven danced a dance for the fled sun.

Dark light dissatisfies. I know
his impure joy, the luminous darkness
of rubbed eyes: feeling I know,
knowing I can only feel.
Momentarily, the heart seems to stop.

The motion begins again, muffled, insistent, a train
seeking its own horizon, but making its journey mean.

IV

If a house consumes the spirit,
dust spiraling downward from stair to stair,
windows shutting with ivy and tall weeds,
ceiling so low we must fall to all four legs,
faucets drawing stagnant green water from the well;

If the potted nasturtiums are swarming with aphids,
the geraniums flecked with smuts on the darkening sills;

If with each step the floor creaks
as though a bit of muscle is torn from bone;

Whatever cripple seeks a Lord,
however slowly,
a Lord finds.

v

I swear, use witchcraft, deceive,
am vomited forth from the whale's mouth.
I walk the sands of the desert watching
for the rough sage, perhaps a cactus, to bloom.
There shall be pure water in the wind, a Lord says.

The heavy man clumping beside me stands,
holds me in his sweating paws and whispers
in a fervor of knowing: "It is enough.
We have come far enough, watched long enough, to die."

Shall we not, gladly, give up our flesh
to the shredding wind?

We shall stretch out our blistered arms to touch
the water that shimmers in a cloud
over the far dunes, blowing closer and closer.
The wind shall shake loose a lightning of thorns,
the sky open like the mouth of a rose.
Adoring, we shall draw near.
In need, we choose a Lord.
We welcome the winds.
A Lord finds.

This day is different.
This is the fourth day.
For three days wind
has rattled the shocks of corn.
For three days the sun
has pressed upon a bird
whose corpse has been

brown as the blowing dirt.
But this is the fourth day.
Today, in air still as a vacuum,
the wren's body hums.
The maggots in the sockets of its eyes
are touched blue, like pale flames.
A tendril of blood

twines about its beak.
Today, unfolding a flower,
the sun kindles, spreads
the wren's feathers.
There are no names for such beauty
as the sun finds here.
The wren can rise no higher.

THE CHINA BULL

I

As if hating its fragilities intact
a red bull glares from a china cup,
black hoofs about to stamp ceramic
splinters, black horns about to gouge
gold ages from the delicate rim circling
over (his clay-feldspar-flint) head.

II

Then should a thin jade scup have swum
around this china cup and kept time
quietly through soft-waved centuries
of water, his fins moving to tides
long known? Would not his green permanence,
his old ocean of eye, have meant the better cup?

III

Once there was a golden bird that flew
from bough to golden bough. He sang
a song of gold that circled a gold sun;
he never ceased to sing and always flew
from golden bough to bough. I grew sick
watching him fly, hearing his golden song.

IV

But bull rings are vitrified to shatter-point
and this red bull is the threat of beauty lost.
Alive, but paralyzed for now in statics
of red and black by lights that filter through
his muscled back, he keeps the heavens up
by horn, holds this cup in art by hoof.

The dew's weight is imperceptible
that gathers like a haze on the dark grass
and darkens imperceptibly the whorl
of threads in which the widow curls to pass

her night. Now the first shaft of sunlight
steers among the blades, touches and drums
taut by drying the edge of her vapor-white
web, now free to the low wind that strums

it alive. Unraveling her legs, hearing
her net sing the music of a dying fly
or violin of a gnat's feeble wing,
she rises to focus her hundreds of cells of eye

upon her field. And yet, within her sharp
geometry of sight, she is not angling
deep enough, or high. It is the harp
of the curved sun that orchestrates the morning.

DRIVING AT DAWN

Driving at dawn past Buffalo
we point to steel mills' stacks
reddening the sky as though
they threaten to set it afire. Hereabouts
soot rains steadily on the shacks
of steelmen and their ashen wives,
once sparks themselves in other lives
that burned a while, but then went out.

A limbo of gray trees and grass, then
a few miles more
and roadsides are green again
under the sun. This arsonist,
rising with matches in his fist,
glaring our windshield's ash on fire,
burns again for the steelmen
who burned like hell for their women.

THE MIND AS GREEN THUMB

*He had considered it possible, in a
certain sense, to spiritualize machinery.*
—HAWTHORNE

*Unless poetry can absorb
the machine, i.e., acclimatize it as
naturally and casually as trees, cattle,
galleons, castles, and all other human
associations of the past, then poetry
has failed of its full contemporary
function.*
—HART CRANE

Think of it this way:
the fan is a black flower.
Bees buzz as it turns
over this table, its garden.
It is metallic and hardy,
not the rose of one summer.

Even when the queen bee
draws her brood away,
it will only rust in an attic,
cellar, or garage,
or in harmless garbagedom
at the dump.

Outside, dandelions choke
the new grass that is rooted
by moles that cut tulip bulbs
from their blind cells. Aphids
swarm the nasturtiums
like measles. Etcetera.

But like a servant planet
it turns to your head,
its sun and center.
Think of it this way:
the fan is a black flower
that kills an occasional fly.

That October I thought: so far, so good.
The dreary cycles of leaves, the predictable
encroachments of evening—these I managed or ignored,
knowing: there are still times when time is still.

One birch (it did not matter it was dead)
affected an innocence to change that fall.
But then, holding its bare branches rigid
and lusterless to the sun, it fell.

Not one day passed but the tree burned
into the weather, nostalgic, memorable
as the words I avoided, the motions of this world.
There was no time when time was still.

Yet, it was as though the weather waited, held
back for one birch, dead, but flammable;
it was as though the low sun delayed
descent, hovered, red and impossible.

THE KING'S MEN

What is it, inside them and undeniable,
that mourns him? that drives them, searching
for the moon-shaped tracks of his horse,
a glint of armor within a maze of pines?

He'd known their barbarous need would never wane;
They will keep on to the next horizon,
where he waits. They will keep on, lowering
their barred visors against the setting sun.

I Visit Washington, D.C.,
Locate the Dead Letter Office
Where Bartleby the Scrivener Worked for a Time,
and Find in the Top-left Drawer of His Desk,
the Heart's Drawer,
a

POSTCARD

My love, the snow is rising.
I have no time to tell you
how empty this house is.
Only my clothes in the closets,
things, having grown thinner,
I cannot wear or own are mine:
a dilemma of suits from all
seasons; shirts that hang
gray-white as ghosts;
and bad poems, my wide,
wrinkled, flowery ties.
Today your Christmas Cactus
lost its last bloom.

Wanting you to walk in, afraid
of the gathering snow,
I am filling the bare, white
spaces of this card.
You must come to tell me some
errands of life still quicken
under the city's winter.
You must come to tell me
where I've sent this from,
to teach me to sign my name,
to know the day it is,
and love, to tell me who
I can send this postcard to.

GRAVITY

Once again, his maples' burnished leaves
are falling, or the trees themselves,

earlier into dark. These nights he wears
his awkward heart out faster,

sleeping on his left side, dreaming
the beat and glide of the migrant starling.

Young in time, his awkward heart,
stoked with the dead and dying, did start

pumping accumulated sludge. Even
bloodless leaves were fuel in season.

He knows no other, better ways
to toll what his awkward heart says.

Too late, old and waiting to die,
   to be curious, wondering, as he lay there,
     where, in the full-branched willow
      did the bird sing. . . .

His eldest son would not circle him three times,
   letting branches fall like altar candles
     on his last sheet. He would be no ghost
      fired to holiness. He would be no ash
       swirled in any river of the world.

Where, in the thick willow, was the bird singing?
   And where was the white tower of the bell's
     first directionless diction?
      If he could know beginnings,
       the precision of places, would it be?
        it would be more like dying in Benares.

THE STADIUM

The stadium is filled,
for this is the third night the moon
has not appeared as even a thin sickle.
We light the candles we were told to bring.
The diamond is lit red with torches.
Children run the bases.

A voice, as though from a tomb,
leads us to the last amen of a hymn.
Whole sections of the bleachers begin to moan.

The clergy files from the dugouts
to the makeshift communion rails
that line the infield grass.

We've known, all our lives,
that we would gather here in the stadium
on just such a night,

that even the bravest among us
would weep softly in the dark aisles,
catching their difficult breath.

At night,
off the Hamptons,
the sky deceives with stars
long burnt out,

shellfish poachers
dig the forbidden waters
off the duck farms,
play hide-and-seek

with lawmen who slide
over the marshes in flat boats
like fish at the ocean's bottom,
one white ray of an eye

mounted on their foreheads.
Here the waters are poison,
the clams thick as diamonds
in the fables of lost mines.

THE SACRAMENT

Once again, good silver and crystal,
a centerpiece of plastic flowers, and linen
from the cedar chest arranged with skill.
With whispered grace we let the year begin.

The tree yet hung, the windows sprayed with snow,
the mantle lined with bottles of empty wine.
A lamp sheds paper mistletoe.
With whispered grace we let the year begin.

The fire of pressed logs, pale as tinsel,
flickers on the turkey's basted skin.
We'd like to find some way to win
the past year, some religious flame to fill

its hide with more than aging flesh and bone.
With whispered grace we enter time again.

TO LIVE IN THE WORLD

I

That tree gave way at last
to the violent, woman-of-a-storm, Nancy,
of just mid-season's alphabet
and just mid-century.

The weight of its great girth
and great branches met
the hurricane-beaten earth
in a way I won't forget:

it did not split, but descended
like fog its whole, vague form
to our back lawn, and bared
an acre of grass to the storm.

Cherry, but all the 'spreading laurel'
of Yeats's poem, and planted in the sand soil
of Long Island to remember,
as legend goes, the birth of a daughter.

II

We chopped, sawed, and carted away
in sunlight and headlight, worked
silent in the dying wind. Those nights we lay
us down to dream, and I'd pretend:

the tree would hover its ghost,
continue its reawakening
to April, refusing to be lost,
refusing to break, continuing to sing:

it still swung the bulb nest
of a pair of orioles returning
their years to an island east
of Eden and north of spring:

it still shook with dark-red fruit
and its leaves yet dripped
their prisms of fine rain, and forgot
that they, and part of us, were dead.

III

This matter of memory runs deep
as earth. Just yesterday I went
down-cellar to raise our burner's heat
against the sudden incident of frost,

and kneeling there, knees to cement
as though in a church damp
as the outer weather, communicant
with webs and crevices, I placed my lamp

against a cracking wall,
and noticed the cherry's roots
had broken through, as though a mole
had burrowed down, or even rats,

or only ropes of eyeless tree.
Whether to strengthen or subdue,
I'll never know. Probably,
and simply enough, both are true.

IV

There are still some photographs.
They'll have to do. But we
are rendered mostly shadows
under influence of tree.

And how will spirit want to say it?
As the cherry was losing, was falling,
the house lightened to fit
the sky, our pupils closing.

But we'd smoke our air of autumn
with its million leaves, and learn
the ways of the world were warm
as body in its quick burn.

The riddle is enough, is enough.
Our earth gave what it could give.
Trees are of knowledge and of life.
Our cherry was of knowledge and of love.

v

A simple thing, a tree that fell,
and falling, allowed light to a house.
Now time still moves through a glass windbell
that survives new scents of spruce,

in a common yard that once,
shaded but sung with birds,
fruited but snowhung and dense
with cold, was yes and no, both words.

Thus this act of balancing memories:
the terrible winter's silhouette it threw
against a house; the flocks of starlings it drew
down from the sky like dark leaves:

but its branches holding the full summer,
shaking brilliant after light rain.
The abstract beauties we remember.
We'll live as though we'd have it fall again.

PRELUDE TO AN EPITAPH

There is no hope of escaping the threatened
punishment by sinking into nothing at death,
like brute creatures.

              —JONATHAN EDWARDS

A dead pet once licked my face in a dream,
and I have seen the spirit of a cat dwell
in a child's heart, ripple a bowl of cream,
but then die, eventually mortal.

I have seen snakes writhe in their cold blood
for days, and rats run headless to their nests,
but these are wholly instinctual episodes.
A dog dies and does not loose a ghost:

a dog dies. Its once shining eyes
lose focus, render the sun gray, where,
memories and future razed, a glaze
of dust settles quickly on its dull stare.

I wish for this nothing, to die beyond belief.
To end like the visible world is enough, is enough.

THE EXHUMATION

He works inexorably at night, spading
the pliant grass and wet earth, holding
to intuition, and, once the earth is broken, smell,
until his spade depresses fur, or clanks on skull.

He must know that spirit goes to the grave.
He hauls the beasts forth as though alive,
pulling on limbs broiling with maggots,
shaking caked dirt from their ears and snouts.

The sockets of the animals' eyes grow
with now the darkness of his full shadow
and now starlight, as he bends to clean
their hides with spit and a waterfall of urine:
he lives to wash animals from the dead.

I've dreamed gratefully of burial and hoped to hide,
but know, if the time comes to a full moon,
if he is more than intimation,
if he has bathed the brilliant beasts of heaven,
I'll have to suffer being washed clean.

THE DEER

As the mountain was falling
I was drawing on the walls of the cave.
I've lived here since the first tremors.

Trees fell across the cave's mouth.
My charcoal deer were flushed green.
Light rippled their flanks like water.

The wind rose and opened the eye of the cave.
Light shone orange through the dust.
My deer pawed the flames.

When the mountain fell I searched
for my deer by the sparks of stones.
I lie here alone in the dark.

THE DARK

I am glad of that other life,
the charcoal I rubbed on the cave's walls,
my deer that moved with the sun
before the mountain fell.

Even though the weather is over
the rain's hoofs clatter.
Even in the cave's dark
the trees' antlers click together.

This is my sleep and a dream,
or my first awakening, or both.
I am glad of my deer.
The dark has many doors.

THE DOORS

I have heard, lying here beyond
measurements of time, the ocean

swelling above this chamber, seeping
down. The cave's roof weeps

cones, horns of lime.
Its floor grows stone columns.

When I lost my eyes I began
to see. Now I am pure, white bone,

fused to the cave's floor.
Blind bats dip and skitter

down from their ledges, where
clouds of white mist gather.

The mist rolls down.
Stone ferns bloom white
on the cave's floor.
My deer walk in woodsmoke,
sip the edges of dark pools.
Vapor rises from fur.

One buck moves near,
licks my ribs from the floor
with his warm tongue.
I have nothing to forgive.
I am glad of my deer,
the life I lived, and live.